MY HUSBAND
CAN'T COOK BOOK

LISA CRAMER

Food Stylists: Lisa Cramer, Kathy Mac Donald and Teri Ford

Editing by: Kathy Mac Donald and Teri Ford

Photography by: Pat Ford, Lisa Cramer

Special thanks to all my friends, family and neighbors who became real full!

ISBN 1-932252-47-9

First Edition
10 9 8 7 6 5 4 3 2

Published by

continuum

1045 N. Armando Street, Suite G
Anaheim, CA 92806
866-799-2738
www.creativecontinuum.com

Dedication

One afternoon I was sitting in the kitchen with my teenage daughter, Britney, and her friends. Having decided they were hungry, they couldn't think of any creative ideas of what to make—even though the fridge and pantry were fully stocked. Suddenly realizing they didn't know anything about cooking, my thought was, "WOW—how times have changed!" These girls didn't know how to be creative, even with the most basic ingredients of simple cooking right under their noses. This instantly inspired me with the idea for a fun cookbook. The purpose of this book is to share some helpful hints and basic (easy) recipes with anyone just moving out of the house and getting started on their own.

I would like to dedicate this book to all the mothers out there who seem to have all knowing answers when it comes to the basics of cooking and being creative in the kitchen. I remember how often I've had to call my own mom, to either ask about a recipe, or be reminded about a measurement. Wanting my own simple recipes to have the same special touches that hers always had, I created this cookbook to make it easier to prepare a variety of simple and delicious recipes.

From my kitchen to yours,

Lisa

To my favorite people.
Enjoy! Lisa Crom

Helpful hints

&

Easy Recipes

From Our Home

to Yours

When You Are

"Out on Your Own"

Table of Contents

Chapter Twelve: My First Turkey Dinner!

Chapter One

FYI for the Kitchen

Helpful Hints
for
Saving Time & Steps

1. Check all ingredients before you start cooking. Make sure you have everything you need.

2. Take all your ingredients out and place them in your cooking area, your utensils also. Chop what needs chopping.

3. Never pour grease down the drain. Pour grease in a empty can, let harden, then place in garbage can.

4. To avoid contamination, always wash your hands, chopping board, and counter tops thoroughly after handling raw meat. It is a good idea to have a spray bottle handy made up with 2 tablespoons of bleach to 1 quart of water. Use for cleaning counter tops and cutting boards or hands.

5. To prevent spoiling, do not leave any foods containing eggs, meat, mayonnaise, or dairy products for more than 2 hours without refrigeration.

6. Before microwaving or cooking in an oven, always make sure that the dish is microwave-proof or oven proof.

7. Do not put metal, some plastic wraps or Styrofoam in the microwave. It will melt and can cause damage.

Measurements	Equivalent
1 Tablespoon	3 Teaspoons
¼ Cup	4 Tablespoons
⅓ Cup	5⅓ Tablespoons
1 Cup	16 Tablespoons
1 Pint	2 Cups
1 Quart	4 Cups (2 Pints)
1 Gallon	4 Quarts (Liquid)

Abbreviations

tbsp or T	tablespoon
tsp or t	teaspoon
c	cup
lb	pound
pkg	package
@	at

Terms in the Kitchen

Crush   =   To press juice out of fruit or force garlic through a press.

Simmer   =   To place on low heat until all ingredients have cooked .

Dice   =   To cut into cubes less than ½ inch.

Boil   =   To heat until bubbles rise and break the surface.

Scald   =   Heating milk until tiny bubbles appear on the sides of the pan.

Julienne =   To cut into lengthwise strips.

Peel   =   To strip off outer layer of skin.

Sauté   =   To lightly brown and heat quickly on high heat.

Broil   =   To melt or brown just the top under a broiler.

Baste   =   Apply juices or flavoring over food during the cooking process.

Garnish =   To use items such as parsley or fruit slices for decoration.

Dash   =   A quick shake (about ¼ tsp)

Stir- Fry =   Small bite size pieces cooked in oil on high heat in a skillet or wok.

Mince   =   To finely chop into very small pieces.

Whisk   =   To stir together using a wire whisk.

Pantry

Flour	Sugar	Brown Sugar
Baking Soda	Baking Powder	Salt & Pepper
Honey	Cornstarch	Rice
Parmesan Cheese	Spaghetti Sauce	Olive Oil
Red Wine Vinegar	Distilled Vinegar	Tuna
Syrup	Assorted Noodles	Bread Crumbs
Vanilla	Spices	Salad Oil
Soda Crackers	Dijon Mustard	Minced Garlic
Olives	Mayonnaise	Tomato Paste
Ketchup	Chocolate Chips	Evaporated Milk
Corn Syrup	Jelly	Shortening
Raisins	Rolled Oats	Taco Seasoning
Onion Soup Mix	Peanut Butter	Hot Sauce
Confectioner Sugar	Worcestershire Sauce	
Red Pepper Flakes	Cream Soups (Any Variety)	
Chicken & Beef Broth	Un-sweetened Cocoa	

Accurate Measuring Tips

Use measuring spoons:
> For measuring liquid and dry ingredients. *

Use measuring cups:
> For measuring dry ingredients.
> (non-liquids).*

Use glass measuring cups:
> For measuring liquids.

For ingredients such as brown sugar;
> Pack firmly into cup.

Shortening: Rinse measuring cup with water, the shortening will slide out easily. If your recipe calls for melted shortening it will measure the same amount as if it was solid.

Bulk measuring: Items such as nuts, cheese, grated coconut, bread crumbs or fruit, pack very tightly for an exact measure.

> * Always use a spatula or knife to level ingredients for an accurate measure.

Common Herbs & Spices

Basil	Add to spaghetti sauces. Use fresh basil in salads, salad dressings and butter spread.
Chives	Use in eggs, salads, meat dishes, sauces and salads.
Cinnamon	Mix with sugar for toast, cookies, and desserts.
Dill	Use in fish dishes, salads, eggs, roasted vegetables and sauces.
Dry Mustard	Use in eggs and sauces.
Garlic powder	Use in eggs, cream cheese spreads and salad dressings.
Nutmeg	Use in fruit desserts, eggs, and cookies.
Oregano	Use in spaghetti sauce, Italian dishes, and chicken.
Paprika	Use to garnish appetizers, eggs, and sauces.
Parsley	Add to herbed cream cheese, garnish almost any dish.

Suggested Items to Start Your Kitchen

Measuring cups & spoons

Tongs

Cheese grater

Wooden spoons

Baking soda (for frig)

Basting brush

Pots & pans (saucepan)

Non-stick fry pan

Blender

Ladle

Ice cube trays

Paring knife

Muffin pan

Cooling rack

Oven mitts

Meat loaf pan

Mixer

Spatula

Cake tester

Scrub brush

Hand towels

Colander

Baster

Funnel

Sharp knives

Scissors

Apple slicer

Vegetable peeler

Baking pan

Bread knife (serrated)

Casserole dish (oblong & square)

Egg poacher

Can Opener

Potato masher

Whisk

Chapter Two

Appetizers

Shrimp & Cream Cheese Dip

1 bottle cocktail sauce
1 cup fresh baby shrimp
1 pkg (8 oz) cream cheese

DIRECTIONS: Place cream cheese on a plate, pour cocktail sauce over top. Top with shrimp. Serve with crackers.

SUGGESTION: Purchase about ¾ pound of shrimp. This leaves a little extra to refresh the dip later on.

Hot Beef Dip

1 pkg chipped beef
1 tsp worcestershire sauce
1 tsp lemon juice
1 tsp garlic salt
2 (8oz) pkgs cream cheese (softened)
¾ cup mushrooms
2 tbsp onion (minced)

DIRECTIONS: Mix cream cheese, worcestershire sauce, lemon juice and garlic salt together in a bowl, add chipped beef (chopped into small pieces). In a separate skillet, add butter and sauté mushrooms and onion until brown. Add to cream cheese mixture. Place in baking dish and bake @ 350° for 20 minutes. Serve with crackers.

SUGGESTION: Can be baked and served in a hollowed out French bread loaf.

Chili Dip

1 can chili
1 (8oz) pkg cream cheese
1 tsp hot sauce

DIRECTIONS: Stir cream cheese and chili together in an ovenproof dish. Bake @ 350° for 20 minutes or microwave until heated thru. Serve with corn chips or tortilla chips.

Artichoke Dip

1 cup sour cream
1 cup mayonnaise
1 cup parmesan cheese
1 can artichokes (chopped and drained)
1 tsp hot sauce

DIRECTIONS: Mix all ingredients together and place in an oven proof dish. Bake @ 350° for 20 minutes, or microwave until heated thoroughly.

SUGGESTION: You may also bake and serve in a hollowed out sourdough round or french bread loaf.

Nachos

1 lb cooked hamburger or chicken	1 bag tortilla chips
1 can black olives	2 tomatoes (chopped)
2 cups cheese (grated)	2 green onions (chopped)

DIRECTIONS: Place chips on a platter. Top chips with cooked meat and layer with remaining ingredients, leaving the cheese for the top. Place platter in a warm 200° oven for about 10 minutes until cheese melts or microwave until warm throughout. Top with sour cream, guacamole, salsa, ranch dip or whatever you desire.

SUGGESTION: Poaching chicken in water instead of frying works well for nachos; it shreds nicely. Place full chicken breasts in pan of boiling water and cook for approximately 15 to 20 minutes. Remove from water and cool. Shred for nachos and season to taste.

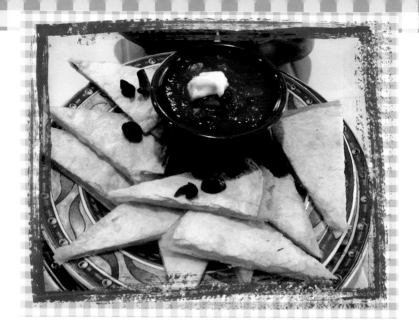

Quesadillas

2 tortilla shells
1 cup monterey jack cheese
1 cup cheddar cheese

DIRECTIONS: Place one tortilla shell on a baking sheet, top with grated cheeses, place second shell on top. Place in oven and bake @ 325° for approximately 5 minutes, watch carefully so it does not burn. Remove from oven. Use a pizza cutter to slice. You may also cook it in the microwave using a dinner plate on maximum heat for approximately 30 seconds until cheese has melted. This can also be done in a frying pan on low heat.

SUGGESTION: Be creative! Add chilies or refried beans, peppers, bacon, olives, chicken, tomatoes and serve with sour cream, salsa, guacamole or ranch dip.

SERVES 1 TO 2.

Potato Skins

3 potatoes (baked)
1 cup cheddar cheese
4 slices bacon (cooked & crumbled)
black olives (sliced)
1 green onion (chopped)

DIRECTIONS: Bake potatoes @ 350° approximately 1 hour, (for medium to large size potatoes). After baking, cut potatoes in half lengthwise. Scrape most of the potato out, leaving a small layer of potato in the skin. Fill shell generously with all other ingredients and bake @ 250° for 10 minutes or until cheese has melted. Serve with sour cream or ranch dip.

SUGGESTION: Be inventive, use whatever topping you like. Sprinkle with garlic powder and parmesan cheese or add seasoned hamburger and cheddar cheese.

Chili Fries

½ lb frozen french fries
1 can chili
cheddar cheese (grated)

Directions: Bake fries as directed on pkg. Top with heated chili and cheddar cheese.

Suggestion: Home fries can be made by cutting a potato lengthwise, placed
on a baking sheet with a small amount of oil drizzled over the top. Salt to
taste. Bake @ 350° for 30 minutes or until potatoes are tender. Top with chili
and cheese.

Shrimp Dip

1 pint sour cream
1 can baby shrimp
1 cup sharp cheddar cheese (grated)
1 tsp yellow onion (minced)

DIRECTIONS: Use a fork to smash and shred shrimp. Mix all ingredients together and chill for 2 hours before serving.

Spinach Dip

1 pkg frozen spinach
1½ cups sour cream
1 cup mayonnaise
1 pkg dry vegetable soup mix
1 can water chestnuts (chopped)
3 green onions (chopped)

DIRECTIONS: Place spinach in colander and squeeze to reduce moisture. Mix spinach, sour cream, mayonnaise, soup mix, water chestnuts, and onion in a bowl. Cover and refrigerate for 2 hours. Serve with crackers.

SUGGESTION: Serve in a hollowed out round of bread. Use inside bread pieces for dipping.

Easy Meatballs

3 lbs hamburger
1 egg
¾ cup bread crumbs
⅓ cup milk
1 onion (chopped)
1 tsp worcestershire sauce
salt & pepper (to taste)
garlic salt

For Sauce: 1 (14oz) bottle ketchup
1 (12 oz) can cola
¼ cup grape jelly (optional)

DIRECTIONS: Mix all ingredients together in a large mixing bowl (except for sauce). Roll into balls and cook in oven on a baking sheet for 20 minutes @ 350°. Place cooked meatballs in saucepan or crock pot. Prepare sauce and pour over meatballs. Cook on medium low heat for 2 hours, or until meatballs are tender.

Little Franks

1 pkg little party franks
1 bottle of barbeque sauce (any kind)
¼ cup grape jelly

DIRECTIONS: Place franks in a skillet. Pour barbeque sauce over franks, and add jelly. Cover and heat for 20 minutes. You can also cook them in a microwave until heated thru.

Beer Cheese Fondue

* 1 cup beer
1 lb (16oz) cheddar cheese (grated)
2 tbsp flour
1 tsp worcestershire sauce
1 tsp dry mustard
1 tsp crushed garlic

DIRECTIONS: Add beer to a saucepan or fondue pot. Boil for 1 minute. Add cheese, flour and all other ingredients; heat until cheese has melted. Add all other ingredients and serve. Serve with torn french bread pieces. Makes about 3 cups.

SUGGESTION: Non-alcoholic beer can be used.

Chapter Three

Breakfast

French Toast

½ cup milk
2 eggs
1 tsp vanilla
4 slices bread

DIRECTIONS: Beat milk, eggs and vanilla together. Lay each slice of bread in milk mixture and let soak for at least 20 seconds on each side. Place on lightly buttered griddle or frying pan. Flip bread after you are sure the bottom side has had a chance to brown. Serve with butter and syrup.

SUGGESTIONS: You can also add cinnamon to milk mixture, use eggnog instead of milk. Raisin bread also makes good french toast. My suggestion is to use french bread for your french toast.

Pancakes

1 egg beaten
¾ cup milk
1 cup flour
2 tbsp vegetable oil
1 tbsp sugar
3 tsp baking powder
½ tsp salt

DIRECTIONS: Mix all ingredients together in a bowl or blender. Rub the surface of your skillet with a little butter or non stick spray. Gently pour approximately 1/3 cup batter onto skillet and cook until bubbles appear on the top of the pancake, then flip. If batter is too thick, add a little more milk or water for the consistency you prefer.

SYRUP RECIPE: Heat together in saucepan:
1 tbsp butter
½ cup each corn syrup & brown sugar.

SERVES 4.

Bagel and Cream Cheese

1 bagel (any flavor)
1 (4oz) cream cheese (softened)

SUGGESTION: You may add salmon, garlic, dill, strawberries, or honey to make interesting flavors of cream cheese to top your bagel.

Serves 1.

Breakfast Sandwich

2 slices bread or English muffin
1 slice ham or (deli ham)
1 egg
1 slice cheese

DIRECTIONS: Top toasted English muffin or bread with fried or scrambled egg. Top with ham and cheese and second slice of bread; warm thoroughly in a skillet or microwave until cheese has melted.

SERVES 1.

Cinnamon Toast

2 slices bread (toasted)
butter
sugar and cinnamon mixture

DIRECTIONS: Butter toasted bread and sprinkle on cinnamon sugar mixture.

SUGGESTION: Always have a sugar mixture already made up in your cupboard. The mixture is equal amounts of sugar and cinnamon. Delicious with hot cocoa.

SERVES 1.

Poached Eggs

DIRECTIONS: Pour ¼ cup water into saucepan, add 1 teaspoon vinegar (This will prevent breakage). Gently add two eggs one at a time cook, 3-5 minutes. Remove eggs from pan with a slotted spoon and drain them briefly on a paper towel.

Fried Eggs

DIRECTIONS: Heat skillet to medium, melt 1 tbsp butter in pan, when butter is melted break the egg into the pan. If you prefer sunny-side up, do not flip. If you prefer over medium, cook on one side then flip. If you prefer well done, break the yolk and cook thoroughly.

Hard Boiled Eggs

DIRECTIONS: Fill saucepan with cold water, place eggs in the pan until water covers the eggs entirely. Add salt—which prevents cracking. Boil for 7 minutes. Remove from heat and run cold water over eggs—this makes the eggs easier to peel.

Scrambled Eggs

DIRECTIONS: Heat skillet on medium heat, add 1 tbsp butter and melt. While butter is melting, crack eggs in a bowl and whip with fork until blended, pour in skillet and stir with spatula until you like the consistency, at this time you may add cheese or anything else you desire.

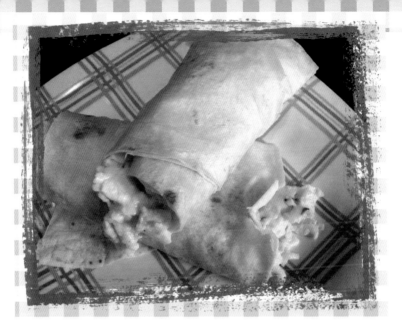

Egg Wrap

1 tortilla
2 eggs (scrambled)
salt & pepper

DIRECTIONS: Warm tortilla, place scrambled eggs in the middle of tortilla. Add meat such as hamburger, bacon, ham, or sausage; add cheese such as cheddar, feta, or Swiss cheese . Roll up tortilla and serve.

SUGGESTIONS: You may also put a spoonful of sour cream inside tortilla for added flavor; or hot sauce.

SERVES 1 .

Blender Quiche

1 pie shell (store bought or homemade) *
3 slices bacon (pre-cooked)
¾ grated cheese (Swiss or cheddar)
3 eggs (beaten)
1 cup cream
1 tsp nutmeg
dash of parsley

DIRECTIONS: Poke holes in bottom of pie shell with a fork. (This helps the shell bake evenly). In blender or mixing bowl, mix together all remaining ingredients. Pour into shell and bake @ 350° for 45 minutes.

* Bake pie shell according to pkg directions.

SERVES 4-6.

Around the World Omelets

3 eggs
1 tbsp water or cream
1 tbs butter

DIRECTIONS: Whip eggs and water together, set aside. Melt butter in a skillet and add egg mixture. Create the omelets you desire, while eggs are cooking on medium heat.

SUGGESTED FILLINGS: Chili and cheddar cheese, diced onion and ham with cheddar cheese, sliced mushrooms, chopped green onions, diced tomatoes, black olives, green or red peppers, salsa. You can also add a drop of hot sauce. Swiss, feta, gorgonzola, American and parmesan cheeses go well with eggs.

SERVES 1.

Hash Browns

3 potatoes (pre-boiled & diced)
1 small green onion (chopped)
½ cup shredded sharp cheese
½ cup diced green or red pepper
½ tsp paprika and onion salt

DIRECTIONS: Place potatoes in a skillet, add 1 tbsp oil.* Cook potatoes until browned. Add onion and red pepper. Sauté until soft. Add paprika and onion salt. Stir in cheese and let it melt. Kielbasa, sausage or ham can be added to make it a full breakfast meal rather than a side dish.

* USE ADDITIONAL OIL IF NEEDED.

Augratin Hash Browns

1 ½ pkg frozen hash browns (block style)
1 ½ cans cream of chicken soup (un-diluted)
1 pint (16oz) sour cream
1 green onion (chopped)
1 cup cheddar cheese (grated)
1 can fried onions

DIRECTIONS: Lay frozen hash browns in the bottom of a casserole dish. Mix together soup (un-diluted), sour cream, green onion and cheese. Heat until combined. Pour over hash browns. Bake @ 350° to 375° for 1 hour. Sprinkle more grated cheese and 1 can of fried onions on top. Place under broiler until browned (watch carefully).

SERVES 8-10.

Coffee Cake

Topping:
2 ½ cups flour
¾ cup sugar
1 cup brown sugar
¾ cup oil
Set aside 1 cup of above mixture for topping.

DIRECTIONS: Add the remaining ingredients to the topping mixture.
½ tsp salt, nutmeg and cinnamon
1 cup buttermilk (or sour milk recipe is below)
1 egg
1 tsp baking soda (mixed with 1 tsp hot water)

Beat well and pour ingredients in greased 13 x 2 x 9 pan. Cover with reserved topping. Bake @ 350° for 20-25 minutes. 1 (8oz) can pineapple bits (strained) can be sprinkled on top before baking.

SERVES 6-8.
* Sour 1 cup milk with 3 tsp lemon juice and let sit for 3 to 4 minutes.

Banana Bread

3 (about 1½ cups) mashed bananas (very ripe)
½ cup shortening
2 eggs
1 cup sugar
2 cups flour
½ tsp salt
1 tsp soda
¼ cup walnuts (optional)

DIRECTIONS: Cream shortening, sugar, soda, salt and nuts together in a large bowl. Add flour and eggs. Add mashed bananas. Mix well and place in medium size bread pan; Bake @ 350° for 35 to 40 minutes. Serve with butter.

MAKES 2 LOAVES.

* Soft Cream cheese is wonderful spread on top in place of butter.

Caramel Coconut Topping

2 tbsp flaked coconut
2 tbsp brown sugar
1 tbsp almonds or crushed walnuts (optional)
2 tbsp butter (softened)

DIRECTIONS: Mix together in small bowl, spread on unbuttered toast or bagel then place under broiler. Watch carefully, this will burn easily.

SERVES 2.

Grandma's Oatmeal

DIRECTIONS: Cook oatmeal according to pkg instructions. Add approximately 2 tbsp evaporated milk in individual bowls and add oatmeal. Mix according to the consistency you desire. Top with brown sugar and a slice of butter.

SUGGESTION: You may also add raisins.

SERVES 1.

Chapter Four

Lunch

Tuna Melt

1 English muffin or bread slice
1 can tuna
⅓ cup mayonnaise or salad dressing
1 slice cheese (American or Cheddar)
1 slice tomato (optional)

DIRECTIONS: Toast muffin or bread slice, place tuna mixture on top, add cheese and tomato. Place under broiler until cheese is melted.

SUGGESTION: You may also add green onion, relish, dill, sweet pickle or radishes to tuna mixture for added flavor.

SERVES 1.

Grilled Cheese Sandwich

2 slices bread
2 slices cheese (American or Cheddar)
butter or margarine

DIRECTIONS: Butter outer sides of both slices of bread. Lay cheese on the inside (non-buttered sides). Heat skillet on medium-high. Place ½ tbsp of butter in skillet. When melted, carefully lay your sandwich in skillet. Flip over when bottom side becomes golden brown.

SUGGESTION: Add ham, pickles, tomatoes or pre-cooked bacon on sandwich before cooking.

SERVES 1.

* If you prefer an open faced cheese sandwich, place a slice of cheese on a piece of toasted bread and set under broiler until cheese is melted (Watch carefully).

Chicken Salad Sandwich

2 cups chicken (poached & chopped)
2 tbsp black olives
½ cup celery (chopped)
⅓ cup mayonnaise (more if desired)
salt & pepper

DIRECTIONS: Place cooked chicken, celery, and black olives in a mixing bowl. Gently mix in the mayonnaise and salt & pepper to taste. Spread on the bread of your choice.

SUGGESTIONS:

Add halved red or green grapes or cashews.

Add small chunks of Swiss cheese.

SERVES 2.

Egg Salad Sandwich

4 eggs (hard- boiled)
2 tbsp hot dog relish
2 tbsp black olives (optional)
¼ to ½ cup mayonnaise
salt & pepper
dash of cayenne pepper (optional)

DIRECTIONS: Mash eggs in medium size bowl. Add relish, black olives, mayonnaise, and salt & pepper. Makes 2 sandwiches. Serve with your choice of bread or toast, also good on English muffins, French roll or bagel.

SERVES 2.

The Famous BLT

½ lb bacon (pre-cooked)
1 tomato (sliced)
lettuce
mayonnaise
4 slices bread

DIRECTIONS: After bacon has been fried and cooled, toast bread. Spread mayonnaise on bread, lay lettuce on top of mayonnaise, add at least 3 strips bacon and sliced tomato.

SUGGESTION: A turkey club may also be made with a "BLT"—just add 4 slices deli turkey. Instead of mayonnaise, substitute thousand island dressing, and add cheddar cheese or avocado slices to both BLT or the turkey club.

SERVES 2.

Chef Salad

1 cup cooked meat (ham, turkey or beef)
¼ (lb) Swiss cheese (cut lengthwise)
¼ (lb) cheddar (cut lengthwise)
4 cups lettuce
½ cup green onions (chopped)
2 sliced hard boiled eggs (optional)
2 tomatoes (cut into wedges)
½ cup black olives (optional)

DIRECTIONS: Place torn lettuce in a bowl. Add all other ingredients. You may use any dressing desired.

SUGGESTION: For a shrimp or crab Louie salad, omit meat, add shrimp or crab and avocado slices. Serve with thousand island dressing and fresh lemon garnish.

SERVES 2

Kraut Dog

6 hot dogs or bratwurst
6 hot dog buns
1 can sauerkraut
cheddar cheese (optional)

DIRECTIONS: Place hot dogs in a saucepan and cover with water. Bring to a boil and cook at least 5 minutes. Top with heated sauerkraut, cheese, diced onion and any other desired condiments.

SERVES 6.

Tuna Macaroni Salad

4 cups macaroni shells
¼ cup chopped red pepper (chopped)
1 cup black olives (chopped)
2 hard boiled eggs (sliced)
½ cup celery (sliced)
1 can tuna (drained)
1 tsp parsley
salt & pepper to taste.
¼ to ½ cup mayonnaise or (desired amount)

DIRECTIONS: Cook shells, drain and cool—run cold water over the noodles to cool faster. Add all other ingredients, adjusting the mayonnaise amount to your taste. Chill.

SERVES 4-6.

Chili Casserole

1¼ cup corn chips
1 medium onion (chopped)
1 (15 oz) can whole corn
1 (15 oz) can black olives (sliced)
1 cup grated cheddar cheese
1 (15 oz) can chili

DIRECTIONS: Layer crushed corn chips in bottom of casserole dish. Combine chili, corn and olives together in medium bowl and mix well. Pour over chips and top with cheese. Bake @ 375° for 20 minutes. When casserole is done, sprinkle cheese on top. Serve with sour cream if desired.

SUGGESTION: Leftover casserole makes a good dip for chips.

SERVES 2

Macaroni and Cheese

1 lb macaroni noodles
½ lb sharp cheddar cheese (grated)
1 tsp salt
2 cups milk
½ cup (crushed) soda crackers (or bread crumbs)
½ cup ham (diced)

DIRECTIONS: Boil macaroni in salted water until tender and drain well. Place macaroni in a casserole dish. In a saucepan on medium heat add cheese, pepper, and milk. Heat together until cheese melts. Pour over macaroni. Sprinkle finely crushed soda crackers or bread crumbs on top and bake @ 375° for 30 minutes. For a twist, add diced ham, crumbled and cooked sausage, or any vegetable you desire.

SUGGESTION: If you prefer a thicker sauce, combine 1 tbsp butter and 1 tbsp flour in a small bowl and mix it together. Drop spoonfuls into sauce and let it melt.

SERVES 6-8

Britney's Clam Chowder

2 potatoes (peeled)
1 can minced clams (with juice)
1 cup half & half cream
1 tbsp butter
2 cans creamed corn
2 slices cooked bacon (cooked & crumbled)

1 small onion (minced)
2 cans evaporated milk
1 tsp parsley
salt & pepper (to taste)
¼ cup cream cheese

DIRECTIONS: Chop potatoes and onion, add to a soup pot. Fill with enough water to cover the potatoes and onion. Boil until potato and onion are tender—do not drain. Add clams with juice and cook 2 minutes. Add evaporated milk and half and half cream, corn, parsley and bacon. Simmer for 10 minutes. Add cream cheese and butter and let them melt into chowder.

SUGGESTION: For thicker chowder, mix equal amounts of flour with soft butter to make a paste. (1 tbsp flour and 1 tbsp butter) Add it to the chowder. Repeat until you reach a desired thickness.

SERVES 6-7.

Barbeque Burgers

1 lb hamburger
1 onion (diced)
½ cup barbeque sauce
1 (6oz) can tomato paste
1 cup ketchup
1 tsp salt & pepper

DIRECTIONS: Brown hamburger and onion in a skillet. Add all other ingredients. Heat and serve on toasted buns or rolls.

SUGGESTION: Add cheese to individual sandwiches. Add corn or hot sauce to meat mixture.

SERVES 2-4.

Pigs in a Blanket

1 pkg pre-made biscuit dough
1 pkg hot dogs
(8oz) block cheddar cheese
bacon (optional)

DIRECTIONS: Slice hot dogs lengthwise, cut cheese in thick lengthwise chunks about the size of your index finger, place cheese inside hot dog and wrap dough around the dog. It is an option to wrap bacon around hot dog in addition to the dough. Bake @ 350° for 15 minutes and serve.

* Baking time may take longer if you choose to use bacon.

Easy Taco Salad

1 head lettuce
1 can chili
½ cup grated cheese
½ cup black olives (optional)
¼ tomatoes (diced)
½ cup crushed tortilla chips
sour cream

DIRECTIONS: Chop two servings of lettuce and arrange in salad bowls. Add ½ to ¾ cups of the heated chili, olives, and tomatoes to salad. Top with grated cheese and sprinkle with crushed tortilla chips; Garnish with sour cream.

SERVES 2.

Chapter Five

Dinner

1. Fettuccini Alfredo

2. Quick Lasagna

3. Spaghetti Sauce
   w/pasta

4. Spaghetti Pie

5. Tuna Noodle Casserole

6. Chicken Enchiladas

7. Chicken & Rice
   w/mushrooms

8. Meatloaf

9. Swiss Steak

10. Stuffed Steak
    w/Bleu Cheese

11. Oven Beef Stew

12. Shepard's Pie

13. French Onion Soup

14. Hamburger Casserole

Fettuccini Alfredo

1 (8oz) pkg fettuccini noodles
1 (8oz) pkg cream cheese (cubed)
½ cup butter
1 ½ cup parmesan cheese
½ cup cream
dash of parsley

DIRECTIONS: Cook noodles according to pkg directions, drain and set aside. In skillet, melt butter over medium heat. Add all other ingredients, heat thoroughly. Add fettuccini to pan and toss to coat. Add shrimp, diced ham or vegetables if you like, and heat thoroughly. Top with additional parmesan cheese.

SERVES 2-4.

Quick Lasagna

1 (10 oz) pkg lasagna noodles (un-cooked)
1 lb hamburger
garlic salt, parsley, & basil (pinch)
2 (6 oz) cans tomato paste
1 (16 oz) can of stewed tomato

DIRECTIONS: For the sauce, fry hamburger, add above ingredients, cook sauce for 20 minutes.

In separate bowl mix:
    3 cups cottage cheese
    2 beaten eggs
    1 ½ CUP parmesan cheese (grated)
    parsley, salt & pepper (to taste)
    1 lb mozzarella cheese (grated & divided in half)

DIRECTIONS: Pour a small amount of the tomato sauce on the bottom of an 9x13 baking dish and spread with spatula. Lay uncooked noodles on top of the meat mixture. Add a layer of the cottage cheese mixture and then mozzarella cheese. Repeat layering, with tomato sauce as your last layer. Top with remaining mozzarella cheese. Bake @ 350° for 35 to 45 minutes.

SERVES 6.

Spaghetti Sauce With Pasta

1 lb ground beef
1 small onion (diced)
1 (16oz) jar spaghetti sauce
1 (2.25oz) can sliced black olives
1 (5oz) can of tomato paste
½ cup red wine (optional)
1 small onion (diced)
Parmesan cheese

DIRECTIONS: Brown hamburger in a skillet and add onion. Add all other ingredients (except parmesan cheese) and simmer for 1 hour. Serve with your choice of pasta and top with parmesan cheese or sautéed mushrooms. Serve with French bread, salad and red wine.

SUGGESTION: Create your own special sauce using your favorite herbs and spices, garlic, or red pepper flakes. Sauce can also be made using (un-diluted) tomato soup and tomato paste, combined with spices, garlic, etc…

SERVES 5-6.

Spaghetti Pie

Crust = (8oz) spaghetti (cooked & drained)
½ cup grated parmesan cheese
1 egg (lightly beaten)
1 lb ground beef (browned & drained)
2 cups bottled spaghetti sauce
1 (8oz) pkg shredded mozzarella cheese
extra parmesan cheese

DIRECTIONS: Toss spaghetti noodles, parmesan cheese and egg together in a large bowl, coat well. Transfer noodles to a 9 inch pie plate, Press along bottom and sides to form a crust. Brown hamburger and add bottled sauce. Pour meat sauce over crust. Sprinkle with mozzarella cheese and top with additional parmesan cheese. Bake @ 350° for 30 minutes until heated thru and cheese has melted. Let stand five minutes before cutting it into slices.

SERVES 5-6.

Tuna Noodle Casserole

1 (8oz) pkg medium size egg noodles
1 cup celery (chopped)
½ cup onion (chopped)
2 tbsp butter (melted)
1 (12oz) can tuna (drained)
1 can cream of mushroom soup (undiluted)
1 (10oz) pkg of frozen mixed vegetables
1 cup milk
¼ tsp salt
¼ cup grated parmesan cheese
1 cup cheddar cheese

DIRECTIONS: Cook noodles according to package directions, drain well and set aside. In a skillet sauté chopped celery and onion in melted butter until tender. In large bowl, add cooked noodles, celery, onion, tuna and next 4 ingredients. Spoon mixture into a lightly greased 2½ - quart casserole dish. Sprinkle with parmesan cheese. Bake (uncovered) @ 375° for 50 to 60 min or until hot and bubbly. Garnish with cheddar cheese.

SERVES 6-8.

Chicken Enchilada

4 chicken breasts
1 (14 oz) can enchilada sauce
2 cups cheddar cheese (divided in half)
1 (2.25 oz) can black olives (sliced)
6 tortilla shells

DIRECTIONS: Poach chicken and cool. Shred chicken into a large bowl, add half of the enchilada sauce, 1 cup of the cheese and olives. Wrap mixture up a in tortilla and place in a baking dish with the seam side down. Pour remaining enchilada sauce over top and sprinkle with remaining cheese. Bake @ 375° for 20 minutes. Serve with sour cream.

SERVES 4-5.

Chicken & Rice with Mushrooms

4 chicken breasts
1 tbsp olive oil
1 pint sour cream
1 can cream of mushroom soup (un-diluted)
2 cups mushrooms (sliced)
1 tbsp minced garlic

DIRECTIONS: In a skillet on medium-high heat, brown chicken on both sides in 1 tbsp olive oil. Remove from skillet and set aside. Reduce to medium heat, add mushrooms and garlic; sauté until soft. Add cream of mushroom soup and sour cream. Place chicken back into skillet. Cover and let simmer for 10 minutes. Serve over white rice or egg noodles. (cooked according to pkg directions).

SERVES 4-6.

Meat Loaf

1 lb hamburger
1 egg
½ cup milk
¾ cup bread crumbs
1 tsp Worcestershire sauce
½ tsp garlic salt
½ tsp parsley
salt & pepper (to taste)

DIRECTIONS: Combine all ingredients in large bowl, mix together well. Place in loaf pan. Shape meat to form of pan. Spread sauce on top. Bake @ 350° for 30 minutes.

SAUCE

In bowl mix ;
Dash of Worcestershire
¼ cup brown sugar
2 tbsp red wine vinegar
1 tbsp mustard
2 tbsp ketchup

SERVES 2-3.

Swiss Steak

¼ cup flour
1 lb boneless chuck steak
2 tbsp vegetable or olive oil
1 medium onion (cut in large wedges)
1 pkg of dry onion soup mix
1 (6oz) can of tomato paste
1 (14oz) can stewed tomatoes
salt & pepper (to taste)

DIRECTIONS: Place oil in a skillet on medium heat. Coat steak thoroughly on both sides with flour. Place in skillet and brown each side until done. Reduce to medium low heat and pour all other ingredients on top of steak. Cover and simmer for 3 hours. (Cooking slowly on low heat for this length of time will make the meat very tender).

SERVES 4.

* You may want to add more water if sauce gets to thick.

Stuffed Steak with Bleu Cheese

1 sirloin steak
½ cup fresh crumbled bleu cheese
salt & pepper (to taste)

DIRECTIONS: Make a slice on one side of the steak and stuff half of the cheese into it. Place steak on broiling pan (or BBQ grill) and cook on both sides. Broil 10 minutes for medium rare, keep a close eye on it until its done to your liking. Top with additional bleu cheese and salt and pepper. Place under broiler until cheese melts.

Oven Beef Stew

4 lbs stew meat
2 tbsp olive oil
3 cups onion
3 medium potatoes
4 slices cut bacon
3 cloves garlic (minced)
2 tsp thyme

3 cans beef broth
1 (14oz) can crushed tomatoes
6 medium carrots
1 (8oz) pkg frozen peas
½ cup mushrooms (optional)
½ cup red wine
1 bay leaf

DIRECTIONS: Add olive oil in a skillet and brown meat, when done place in oven proof stew pot. Add onions and bacon to same skillet and sauté until onions are slightly brown. Add garlic and sauté for 1 minute. Add thyme, bay leaf, beef broth and stewed tomatoes. Let simmer for at least 3 minutes. Remove from heat and set aside. Chop carrots and potatoes and add to stew pot. Pour broth over meat and vegetables, mix well. Place in oven for 3 hours @ 350°. About 10 minutes before serving add frozen peas and mushrooms and place back in oven.

SUGGESTION: Adding ½ cup red wine gives the stew a nice rich flavor.

Shepard's Pie

1 lb hamburger (browned)
2 cans creamed corn
8 cups mashed potatoes
1 cup cheddar cheese (grated)

DIRECTIONS: Brown hamburger in a skillet, drain fat and place in a 9 x 13 baking dish. Pour creamed corn over hamburger; spread mashed potatoes over corn and sprinkle with cheddar cheese. Bake @ 350° for 30 minutes.

SUGGESTION: Top with sour cream, butter or gravy. You can also substitute 2 cans alphabet soup (un-diluted) for the creamed corn.

Easy French Onion Soup

¼ stick butter
4 cups sliced onions
2 cans beef broth
1 ½ cups water
1 bay leaf

2 tbsp dry sherry (optional)
¼ tsp thyme
4 slices French bread
parmesan cheese (grated)
½ lb Swiss cheese (sliced)

DIRECTIONS: In a soup pot, melt butter and add onions. Cook about 15 minutes until onions are soft. Add broth and next four ingredients. Increase heat and bring to a boil. Reduce heat and simmer. Before serving add sherry. Broil bread on both sides, place in bottom of medium size oven proof bowls. Place bowls on baking sheet or tray. Spoon soup into bowls until just below the rim. Top with slices of swiss cheese and sprinkle with grated parmesan cheese. Place under broiler until cheese melts and is golden brown. Serve with salad.

SERVES 2-4.

Hamburger Casserole

1 lb hamburger (browned)
1 cup celery (diced)
½ cup onion (diced)
1 (10 oz) can cream of chicken soup (un-diluted)
1 (10 oz) can cream of mushroom soup (un-diluted)
½ cup white rice (un-cooked)

DIRECTIONS: Add hamburger, celery and onion together in a skillet. Brown until hamburger is cooked and onions and celery are soft. Transfer to casserole dish. Add the (un-diluted) soups and rice, mix well. Cover and bake @ 350° for 1 ½ hours.

SERVES 4-6 .

Chapter Six

Desserts

Fudge Pie

1 stick (4oz) un-salted butter
2 (2oz) squares unsweetened chocolate
2 eggs (lightly beaten)
1 cup sugar
¼ cup flour
¼ tsp salt
2 tsp vanilla extract
1 pre-baked pie shell (regular or graham cracker)

DIRECTIONS: Preheat oven @ 350°. In small heavy saucepan, combine butter and chocolate. Cook over low heat, stirring occasionally. When melted remove from the heat and cool. In medium bowl, whisk together the eggs, sugar, flour, salt and vanilla. Beat until smooth. Stir in the melted chocolate and blend well. Pour into (pre-baked) pie shell and bake 30 to 40 minutes, or until center is set. It should give a little when you touch it, but should not be liquid. Serve with whipped topping.

SERVES 6-8.

Kathy's Apple Crisp

½ cup brown sugar
½ cup oatmeal (un-cooked)
½ cup flour
½ cup butter (cold)
¾ tsp cinnamon
¾ tsp nutmeg
4 large apples (peeled golden delicious or any yellow apple)

DIRECTIONS: Mix dry ingredients together, crumble in cold butter and mix well, coating all the butter pieces. Slice apples in 9 x 9 baking dish. Top with brown sugar and butter mixture. Dot with additional butter. Bake @ 350° for 30 minutes.

SUGGESTION: Serve with vanilla ice cream.

SERVES 4-6.

Punch Bowl Cake

1 can blueberry pie filling
1 can cherry pie filling
1 large tub whipped topping
1 pkg instant vanilla pudding (pre-made)
1 white cake (pre-baked)
vanilla wafers

DIRECTIONS: With this recipe you will need a punch bowl or a very large serving bowl. Make pudding according to pkg directions and set aside. In the bottom of the bowl take ½ of the baked cake and break it into chunky pieces. Spread half of vanilla pudding over cake, layer one can of pie filling, spread whipped topping on top then start again. Repeat cake, pudding, filling and whipped topping. I like to end with the whipping cream and crush vanilla wafers on top. Decorate with vanilla wafers lining the perimeter of the bowl. Keep Refrigerated.

*THIS MAKES A LOT! IT IS GOOD FOR A LARGE GATHERING,
AND TASTES GREAT TOO!*

Banana Split

1 large banana
any flavor ice cream
hot fudge sauce
crushed pineapple
whipping cream
nuts

DIRECTIONS: Cut banana to accommodate whatever dish you are using. Pile all the other goodies on top of the ice cream and banana. Be creative, anything goes! Candy bits, caramel sauce, strawberries or peanuts are good too.

Chocolate Chip Cookie and Ice Cream Sandwich

2 chocolate chip cookies
½ cup soft ice cream

DIRECTIONS: For a quick and easy treat, take 2 cookies, place softened ice cream in-between. Place on a plate and set in freezer for a few minutes until ice cream is frozen. You may do this with any flavor cookie or ice cream you prefer.

SUGGESTION: Peanut butter cookies w/chocolate ice cream
Sugar Cookies w/chocolate chip mint ice cream
Coconut cookies w/ praline ice cream
Chocolate sugar cookie w/strawberry ice cream

SERVES 1.

* Homemade cookies make the best ice cream sandwiches.

Brownie alá Mode

1 large brownie
vanilla ice cream (softened)
chocolate or fudge sauce (1 jar)
sliced almonds (almonds)

DIRECTIONS: Prepare brownie mix according to package directions. Home-made brownies are even better! Let ice cream stand for a few minutes outside of freezer until ice cream is soft. Cut out a large brownie square and place on a plate. Scoop ice cream on top of brownie and drizzle with chocolate sauce. Add almonds and top with a cherry!

SERVES 1.

Chocolate Fondue

2 cups (12oz) semi-sweet chocolate chips
¾ cup marshmallows (mini)
1 cup heavy cream
¼ tsp vanilla

DIRECTIONS: Melt chocolate chips and cream together in a fondue pot or saucepan. When melted, add marshmallows and vanilla. Serve warm by heating for 10 minutes. Serve with variety of fruit such as pineapple, oranges, bananas, or sliced strawberries.

SUGGESTION: Pretzels or cubed pound cake make great dippers as well.

Creamy Chocolate Dip

½ (8oz) pkg cream cheese (softened)
¼ cup powered sugar
1 tbsp (un-sweetened) cocoa
¼ cup sour cream or plain yogurt
1 tbsp milk
½ tsp vanilla flavoring

DIRECTIONS: Beat cheese at medium speed, add remaining ingredients and mix well. Cover and chill.

SUGGESTION: Serve with assorted fruit such as: strawberries, bananas, oranges, raspberries and pineapple etc…

MAKES ABOUT 1 CUP.

Chapter Seven

Classic Cookies & Bars

Toffee Bars

½ cup butter
½ cup brown sugar
½ tsp vanilla
1 cup sifted flour
1 (6oz) pkg chocolate chips

DIRECTIONS: Cream butter, sugar and vanilla together. Add flour and mix well. Stir in chocolate chips. Press mixture into un-greased 8 x 8 pan. Bake @ 350° for 25 minutes. Cool and cut into small bars.

Chocolate Brownies

2 (3oz) squares un-sweetened chocolate
⅓ cup shortening
1 cup sugar
2 eggs
¾ cup flour
½ tsp baking powder
½ tsp salt
1 tsp vanilla
½ cup (crushed) almonds (optional)

DIRECTIONS: Melt chocolate in a microwave safe dish, medium power, cool. Wisk sugar and eggs together in separate bowl, add melted chocolate. In a separate bowl, stir together flour, baking powder and salt. Mix dry ingredients into the chocolate mixture, add vanilla and almonds. Spread batter into greased 8 x 8 x 2 inch pan. Bake @ 350° for 30 to 35 minutes.

* MAKES ABOUT 12 BROWNIES.

Dream Bars

Crust = 1 cup dark brown sugar
        2 cups flour
        1 cup butter (2 sticks)

Filling = 2 cups brown sugar
        4 eggs
        1 tsp baking soda
        ½ tsp salt
        1 cup coconut
        4 tbsp flour

DIRECTIONS: Spray a 9 x 13 baking pan with non-stick spray, set aside. Mix crust ingredients together and press flat into the baking pan. Bake for 8 to 10 minutes. Mix filling ingredients together and spread mixture over the top of the baked crust. Bake @ 350° for 20 minutes. Bake until light brown. Shake pan to check center for doneness (shake the pan to make sure it is completely cooked and does not "jiggle" in the center).

MAKES 8-10 BARS.

Scottish Shortbread

¾ cup butter
¼ cup sugar
2 cups flour

DIRECTIONS: Cream butter and slowly add the sugar until dough mixture becomes light and fluffy. Gradually add flour and knead dough about 15 minutes until dough becomes smooth and creamy. Roll into an 8 inch round. Press around the edge with your thumb to form a thumbprint decoration. Bake @ 300° for 20 minutes. Reduce the temperature @ 275° and bake for 40 minutes. Cool and cut into wedges like a pie.

SUGGESTION: For an added touch, dip half of the baked cookie into melted chocolate chips.

Oatmeal Chocolate Chip Cookies

1 cup soft shortening
1 cup white sugar
1 cup brown sugar
1 egg
2 tbsps molasses
1 (12oz) pkg semi-sweet chocolate chips

1½ cup sifted flour
1 tsp baking powder
1 tsp cinnamon
1 tsp baking soda
1 cup oatmeal (quick oats)

DIRECTIONS: Cream shortening, sugar, egg and molasses together. In a separate bowl, mix all dry ingredients together except for oats and chocolate chips. Add dry ingredients gradually to creamed mixture. Add chips and oats, mix well. Bake @ 350° for 10 minutes.

SUGGESTION: These cookies make a good ice cream sandwiches (see dessert chapter).

MAKES ABOUT 2 DOZEN COOKIES.

Snickerdoodles

2 cups shortening
3 cups sugar
4 eggs
5½ cups flour (sifted)
4 teaspoons cream of tarter
2 teaspoons baking soda
1 tsp salt

DIRECTIONS: Preheat oven to 350°. With a mixer, cream shortening, sugar and eggs together. Slowly add all dry ingredients and mix well. Roll into medium size balls, roll in sugar and place on an un-greased cookie sheet. Bake @ 350° for 10 minutes until light brown but still somewhat soft (for a chewy cookie).

SUGGESTION: Mix cinnamon into the sugar mixture, or frost them with your favorite frosting.

MAKES 2 DOZEN.

Fancy Peanut Butter Cookies

1¾ cup flour
½ cup sugar
1 egg
1 cup brown sugar
½ tsp baking soda
1 tsp vanilla

½ cup toffee bits (optional)
½ cup butter flavored shortening
½ tsp salt
2 tbsp milk or cream
½ cup peanut butter
chocolate chunks

DIRECTIONS: Preheat oven @ 375. Combine all dry ingredients in one bowl and set aside. Cream together all other ingredients. Add dry ingredients to the creamed mixture. Roll into balls, roll in sugar, coating the ball. Place on a cookie sheet. Bake @ 350° for 10-12 minutes. Immediately top with desired chocolate chunks (white or dark) as cookies are cooling.

MAKES 2 DOZEN.

Chapter Eight

Poor Person's Delicacies

1. Dean's Beef & Bean Dish

2. Hamburger Stroganoff

3. Bake Potatoe Galore

4. Pizza On A Budget

5. Hamburger French Dip

6. Graham Cracker Snacks

7. Chicken Soup

8. Dad's Sunday Hash

9. Fried Rice

10. Grandpa Howard's Midnight Snack

11. Gramma Dorthy's Midnight Snack

12. Crock Pot Suey

13. Popcorn Toppings

Dean's Beef & Bean Dish

2 (15 oz) cans pork & beans
1 lb hamburger

DIRECTIONS: Brown hamburger in a skillet. Add pork & beans and heat thoroughly.

SUGGESTION: You may also add onions. Fry them along with the hamburger. Dean likes his beans with ketchup or barbeque sauce squeezed on top.

SERVES 2.

Hamburger Stroganoff

1 lb hamburger
1 cup dill pickles (chopped)
1 can cream of mushroom soup (un-diluted)
1 cup sour cream
1 pkg egg noodles (cooked)

DIRECTIONS: Brown hamburger, add undiluted can of soup, sour cream and dill pickles. Cook on medium heat for approximately 10 minutes. Serve over egg noodles.

SUGGESTION: This sauce can also be served over white rice.

SERVES 5-6.

Baked Potatoes Galore

Large Baked Potatoes

DIRECTIONS: Before baking always pierce the potato with a fork or knife to let the steam escape. This prevents the potato from exploding. Bake @ 350° for 1 hour. After the potato is baked try some of these ideas for filling.

* chili, cheddar cheese, green onion and sour cream
* bacon, green onion, cheddar cheese and sour cream
* bacon, canned sweet peas, cheddar cheese and sour cream
* diced tomatoes, cooked hamburger, green onion, red peppers guacamole, and salsa .

Pizza on a Budget

tortilla rounds
½ cup cheddar cheese (grated)
½ cup mozzarella cheese (grated)
½ cup mushrooms
½ cup cooked hamburger
1 can tomato paste
½ cup black olives

DIRECTIONS: Place tortilla shells on baking sheet or round cake pan and cover with tomato paste. Layer other ingredients. Bake @ 350° for approximately 15 minutes, or until cheese melts.

* These are just a few ideas for toppings. You can add anything you wish—it's your own pizza after all!

Hamburger French Dip

French bread roll
½ pound hamburger (cooked)
2 slices cheese
1 pkg Au Jus sauce mix

DIRECTIONS: Shape hamburger to fit the roll. Broil or brown the meat in a skillet. Follow directions on the pkg to prepare Au Jus sauce. Heat roll ,place cooked hamburger and cheese slices on the roll and place under broiler, remove when cheese has melted. Dip your sandwich in Au Jus sauce.

SUGGESTION: Sautéed onions and red peppers stuffed into the sandwich are also good. Pepper jack, American or sharp cheddar cheese are recommended.

SERVES 1.

Graham Cracker Snacks

1 pkg graham crackers
1 can frosting

DIRECTIONS: Place frosting in middle of two graham crackers, that's it! If you don't have any canned frosting, here are some simple recipes.

Butter Vanilla Frosting
3 cups confectioners sugar
⅓ cup butter (softened)
2 tsp vanilla
2 tbsp evaporated milk

Mix powdered sugar and butter
Stir in vanilla and milk, beat until smooth.
Makes enough for 13 x 9 cake.

Dark Fudge Frosting
6 tbsp unsweetened cocoa
⅓ cup butter (softened)
2 tbsp milk or cream
2 cups confectioners sugar
1½ tsp vanilla

Mix butter and chocolate. Stir in sugar. Beat in vanilla and milk until frosting is smooth. Makes enough for 13 x 9 cake.

Chicken Soup

2 (14oz) cans chicken broth
3 chicken breasts (poached & shredded)
½ cup carrots (sliced)
½ cup celery (sliced)
½ onion (chopped)
1 tsp garlic salt
3 cups (uncooked) wide egg noodles
salt & pepper (to taste)

DIRECTIONS: Poach chicken in water, cool and shred. Heat the chicken broth, add all other ingredients including shredded chicken. Salt & pepper to taste. Cook on low heat for approximately 2 hours.

SERVES 4-5.

Dad's Sunday Night Hash

left over roast, steak or hamburger
left over vegetables such as green beans or corn
onions
leftover potatos
spices
2 eggs (beaten)

DIRECTIONS: Add oil to skillet on medium heat. Chop and sauté all chosen ingredients together, add spices. Add beaten eggs and cook until done. Top with sour cream or grated cheese.

SUGGESTIONS: This recipe is usually made with leftovers from the previous weeks menu but fresh or frozen vegetables are also good. Be creative.

Fried Rice

2 tbsp olive oil
2 cups cooked white rice
½ cup green onion (chopped)
2 eggs (whipped)
½ cup frozen peas
½ cup carrots (cut thinly)
3 tbsp soy sauce
chicken, shrimp, or pork (optional)

DIRECTIONS: In a skillet on medium heat add olive oil, rice and all other ingredients, except for the eggs. Cook for about 20 minutes. Whip eggs separately. Scrape rice mixture in skillet to one side and pour in eggs. Cook until scrambled and then break them into separate pieces. Mix into rice mixture.

SERVES 6.

Grandpa Howard's Midnight Snack

2 slices bread (toasted dark)
cheddar cheese (sharp)
onion slices (sliced thin)

DIRECTIONS: Toast bread until dark but not burned. Slice sharp cheese (thick), and lay on toast, then layer onion (optional). Top with second slice of toast. Slice in half. Dip each bite into Worcestershire sauce until sauce on plate soaks into bread. Try this, you'll be surprised how good it is!

SERVES 1.

Grandma Dorothy's Midnight Snack

1 slice white bread
jam (any kind)
whipped cream

DIRECTIONS: Spread bread with jam, place whipped cream on top of jam layer. Eat as an open face sandwich.

**** Kids love this sandwich! ****

Crock Pot Suey

2 cups chopped celery
2 cups chopped onions
2 cans bean sprouts (with juice)
2 cans stewed tomatoes (with juice)
2 heaping tbsp Worcestershire sauce
2 heaping tbsp soy sauce
salt & pepper (to taste)
1 lb ground hamburger (browned)

DIRECTIONS: In a stew pot or crock pot add all ingredients and let cook for at least 3 hours.

Popcorn

DIRECTIONS: Pop popcorn, or use natural flavor microwave popcorn. Drizzle butter over popcorn and sprinkle with your topping choice.

SUGGESTED TOPPINGS:
- butter (melted)
- parmesan cheese
- garlic salt
- cinnamon and sugar mixture with melted butter
- cayenne pepper

Chapter Nine

Sauces & Dressings & Spreads

1. Four Different Salad Dressings

2. Meat Marinade

3. Teriyaki Sauce

4. Fresh Fruit Dip

5. Fresh Salsa

6. Horseradish Sauce/ Dill Sauce

7. White Sauce/Cheese Sauce

8. Crostini Spreads

Dijon Dressing

3 tbsp red wine vinegar
1 tbsp olive oil
1 tbsp water
2 tsp Dijon mustard
½ tsp salt & pepper

DIRECTIONS: Wisk together and serve.

1,000 Island Dressing

½ cup mayonnaise
¼ cup ketchup
1 tbsp sweet relish

DIRECTIONS: Mix well… adjust measurements to taste.

Oil & Vinegar

Equal parts: salad oil & red wine vinegar

DIRECTIONS: Mix together in a jar and shake well.

Sweet French Dressing

Equal parts:
ketchup
salad oil
sugar
vinegar

DIRECTIONS: Mix together in a jar and shake well. Chill for 30 minutes.
½ cup measure makes quite a bit!

Meat Marinade

¾ cup salad oil
⅓ cup soy sauce
¼ cup vinegar
2 tbs Worcestershire sauce
1 tsp dry mustard
1 tbsp garlic (more if desired)
2 tbsp fresh lemon juice

DIRECTIONS: Combine all ingredients. Pour over desired meat and let marinate for at least an hour, or overnight.

MAKES ABOUT 1 ½ CUPS.

Teriyaki Sauce

¼ cup soy sauce
½ cup sugar
1 tbsp Marin or rice vinegar
¼ tsp ground ginger
2 cloves garlic (crushed)

DIRECTIONS: Combine ingredients in saucepan and bring to a boil for 2 to 3 minutes, stirring constantly. Refrigerate for 2 hours.

MAKES ABOUT 1 CUP.

* Marin can be found in the Ethnic foods section of the grocery store.

Fresh Fruit Dip

1 cup sour cream
1 tbsp orange juice (concentrate, straight out of can)
1 tbsp honey
Pinch of cinnamon

DIRECTIONS: Mix together as a dip for fresh fruit or as a dressing for a fresh fruit salad.

MAKES 1 CUP.

Fresh Salsa

4 cups tomatoes (chopped and peeled)
2 cups green pepper (chopped)
1 cup jalapeño pepper (chopped) *
1 clove garlic (chopped)
1 whole onion (chopped)
1½ cup cider vinegar
salt to taste

DIRECTIONS: Boil in saucepan for 20 minutes. Chill for about 2 hours before serving.

* Wear gloves when seeding the peppers so you don't accidentally touch your eyes!

Dilled Horseradish Sauce

¾ cup sour cream
½ cup mayonnaise
¼ tsp salt
¼ tsp white pepper
2 tbsp prepared horseradish (grated style)
1 tbsp fresh dill (chopped), or 1 to 2 tsp (dried)

DIRECTIONS: Combine all ingredients together and chill for approximately 2 hours. Serve with steak or prime rib.

SUGGESTION: For a simple sauce for fish, omit the horseradish and pepper and add a squeeze of lemon.

MAKES 1 ½ CUPS.

White Sauce

1 cup hot milk
1 tbsp butter
1 tbsp flour
pinch of salt
pinch of white pepper

DIRECTIONS: In saucepan on medium-low heat, melt butter, add flour and use fork to whisk together making a paste texture. At this stage, add milk slowly, still stirring briskly (this helps to prevent lumps). Cook on medium heat until sauce thickens.

SUGGESTION: You may want to use white pepper instead of black in your white sauce to avoid unattractive specks. Also, 1 cup of cheddar cheese and ½ tsp dry mustard added to above recipe will make a great cheese sauce.

MAKES ABOUT 2 CUPS.

Crostini Spreads

Bleu cheese
1 tsp Olive oil
1 pkg French bread baguettes
1 (4 oz) pkg bleu cheese
2 tbsp red wine
¼ cup cream cheese (softened)
2 tbsp walnuts or pine nuts (crushed)

Spaghetti Sauce & Feta
1 pkg baguettes (toasted)
olive oil
1 cup spaghetti sauce
(homemade or jarred)
1 (3oz) bar feta cheese
(squared or crumbled)

DIRECTIONS: Place breads on baking sheet and brush lightly with olive oil. Place in oven @ 200° to toast breads until lightly browned. Remove toasted bread from oven and spread mixture on baguettes. Place under broiler until cheese melts. Serve immediately.

When preparing spaghetti sauce and feta, place small chunks of feta on top of sauce before placing under broiler. Makes about a cup of bleu cheese mixture.

Chapter Ten

Backyard Barbeque

1. Deviled Eggs

2. BBQ Sauce

3. Shish Kabobs

4. Garlic Butter On The Cob

5. Lisa's Potato Salad

6. Vegetables

7. Mom's Beans

8. Pasta Salad

9. Mint Pie

Deviled Eggs

6 eggs (hard boiled)
mayonnaise
pickles, minced (dill or sweet)
salt & pepper
paprika

DIRECTIONS: Cut hard boiled eggs in half (lengthwise) and place the inner yolk in a bowl. Place halved whites on a plate. Smash yolks with a fork and add all other ingredients to taste (except paprika). Add as much mayonnaise as you would like, until you get the right consistency. Spoon into eggs and sprinkle paprika over top. Chill

* You may also add black olives, shrimp, cayenne pepper or any broken egg pieces.

BBQ Sauce

½ cup ketchup
¼ cup vinegar
2 tbsp onion (diced)
1 garlic cloves (crushed)
1 tbsp Worcestershire sauce
2 tbsp brown sugar
¼ tsp dry mustard

DIRECTIONS: Combine all ingredients together and heat to a simmer, stirring constantly for about 10 minutes.

MAKES ABOUT 1 CUP.

* You can also spice it up with red pepper flakes or cayenne pepper. Brush on chicken or steak before placing on grill and baste the meat with additional sauce as it's cooking.

Shish Kabob

Shish kabobs are a combination of meat, chicken, seafood and vegetables, skewered and placed on the barbeque.

Meats can be marinated, or brushed with your favorite barbeque sauce. Chicken is good marinated in Italian salad dressing. Seafood, such as shrimp, can be brushed with garlic butter.

DIRECTIONS: Alternate meat and vegetables on the skewer. These are some suggestions for vegetables that do well on the barbeque;

  onion wedges
  large cherry tomatoes
  red or green bell pepper chunks
  mushrooms (whole)
  Potatoes wedges (pre-cooked)
  Place skewers on grill, and cook until meat is to desired doneness.

SUGGESTION: Vegetables are also good marinated in Italian dressing before skewering.

Garlic Butter Rub for Corn on Cob

½ cube butter
2 cloves garlic (crushed)
Pinch of parsley
4 ears of corn in the cob

DIRECTIONS: Mix butter and crushed garlic together. Peel corn husks down on the ears (do not fully remove). Rub butter on each ear, cover thoroughly. Take husk and re-wrap the ears. (This keeps corn moist and butter will melt into the ears of corn). Place on grill for 15 minutes until fully cooked. Remove the husks from the cob and dig in!

Lisa's Potato Salad

10 potatoes (peeled, cooked & cut)
1½ cup mayonnaise
3 hard boiled eggs
1 cup celery (sliced)
1 cup dill pickles (chopped)
⅓ cup pickle juice

1½ tsp celery salt
1 cup sliced black olives
salt & pepper to taste
3 large radishes (optional)
dash of mustard (optional)
paprika

DIRECTIONS: Boil potatoes in salted water. (Potatoes cook quicker if cut in half). When done, drain and let cool. Cut up all other ingredients and mix in a bowl. Add cut potatoes into mixture, be careful not to break up potatoes as you mix. Add a dash of mustard if you like and sprinkle with paprika. Chill and serve.

SERVES 8-10 DEPENDING ON SERVING SIZE.

Vegetables on the Grill

Combine any vegetables that you like. This is my favorite combination;
- 2 carrots (sliced)
- 1 summer squash (sliced)
- 1 zucchini (sliced)
- ½ pkg green pea pods
- ½ cup onion (chopped)
- 1 (7oz) can of sliced water chestnuts
- ¼ cup soy sauce
- ¼ cup olive oil
- 2 tsp garlic
- salt & pepper

DIRECTIONS: Place vegetables in mixing bowl, add olive oil, soy sauce, garlic, salt and pepper. Toss until vegetables are coated. Place in foil and seal tightly. Place on barbeque for 20 minutes until vegetables are cooked but not soggy.

SERVES 4-6.

Mom's Baked Beans

2 (28oz) cans of pork and beans
¼ cup molasses
½ cup brown sugar
1 tsp dry mustard
½ cup ketchup (or to taste)
1 tsp garlic (minced)
1 strip bacon (raw and cut)
1 small onion (chopped)

DIRECTIONS: Drain juice from cans (saving juice from one can only). Pour all beans in casserole dish. Add the juice from 1 can only. Mix all ingredients with beans and cook for about 3 hours. Bake @ 300°, depending on your oven's personality—not too hot or beans will be mushy!

SERVES 8-10 .

Pasta Salad with Artichokes

1 pkg spiral noodles
1 bottle Italian dressing
1 can black olives (sliced)
12 cherry tomatoes (cut in half)
1 can or jar marinated artichokes (chopped)
1 cup cubed cheese (desired flavor)

DIRECTIONS: Cook pasta. Add all other sliced and cut ingredients. Mix in dressing well and chill.

SERVES 8-12.

Chocolate Mint Pie

2 cups crushed chocolate cream sandwich cookies
¼ cup butter (melted)
¼ cup milk
1 (7oz) jar marshmallow cream
add peppermint flavoring to taste (1 or 2 drops) *
1 or 2 drops green food coloring *
2 cups whipped topping

DIRECTIONS: Combine crumbs and butter, press into bottom of 9 inch pie pan. Chill until crust is firm. In separate bowl gradually add milk to marshmallow cream. Mix well. Add peppermint flavoring and food coloring, fold in whipped topping. Pour into pan and sprinkle additional crushed cookie crumbs on top. Freeze until firm about 3 hours.

SUGGESTION: Be careful when adding the peppermint extract and food coloring. Add one or two drops at a time and taste test until you are happy with the result. It is very easy to add too much and ruin the pie.

SERVES 8.

Chapter Eleven

Gourmet Dinner for Two

1. Stuffed Mushrooms

2. Shrimp Scampi

3. Peg's Caesar Salad Dressing

4. Rosemary Potatoes

5. Roasted Asprargus W/ Balsamic Vinegar

6. Spicy Biscuits

7. Chocolate Mousse

Stuffed Mushrooms

15 to 20 mushroom caps (stems removed)   ¼ cup bacon (chopped)
½ onion (chopped)   1 cup chicken broth
2 tbsp butter   ½ cup Swiss cheese (chopped)
1 cup seasoned stuffing mix   salt & pepper (to taste)
½ cup prosciutto ham (diced)   1 cup sour cream

DIRECTIONS: Clean and remove stems from mushrooms. Take a spoon and gently scrape the mushroom cap just enough to make a wide opening at top. Chop up the stem pieces and scrapings from the caps, and place them in a skillet along with the onions, bacon, ham and butter; sauté for 2 minutes. Add stuffing mix and chicken broth, mix well. Add salt & pepper and sour cream. Mix well and add the Swiss cheese. When cheese is thoroughly melted, place a spoonful on individual caps, and place on baking sheet. Bake @350° for about 20 minutes. Serve immediately.

SUGGESTION: You can fill mushroom caps ahead of time and refrigerate.

Shrimp Scampi

¼ cup butter
2 tbsp olive oil
12 large or medium shrimp (pre-cooked)
1 tbsp garlic (minced)
1 tsp parsley
salt & pepper (to taste)

DIRECTIONS: Place shrimp in skillet with olive oil, butter and garlic. Sauté for at least 2 minutes until all shrimp is well coated in seasonings and heated thru. Sprinkle parsley over top, and salt and pepper. Just before serving, squeeze a wedge of fresh lemon over top.

SUGGESTION: Serve with French bread to dip in scampi sauce. Serve over white rice, or toss with fettuccini noodles.

SERVES 2.

Peg's Caesar Salad Dressing

¼ cup lemon juice
½ cup olive oil
½ cup parmesan cheese
2 cloves garlic (to taste)
1 tbsp Worcestershire sauce
1 tbsp Dijon mustard
2 tbsp red wine vinegar
Pepper (to taste)

DIRECTIONS: Wisk all ingredients together, this dressing is best when chilled at least an 1 hour or over night. You may also keep it refrigerated up to a week. Serve over romaine, with croutons, parmesan cheese and anchovies for a classic Caesar salad.

MAKES ABOUT 1 CUP.

Rosemary Roasted Potatoes

2 tbsp olive oil
10 red potatoes (cubed)
1 tbsp fresh rosemary (crushed)
salt & pepper

DIRECTIONS: Sauté potatoes in oil until brown. Place potatoes in an oven-proof baking dish, sprinkle rosemary over top, salt and pepper. Place in oven, bake @ 350° for 25 to 30 minutes, stirring occasionally.

SERVES 5-6 .

Roasted Asparagus

1 lb asparagus
balsamic vinegar
coarse salt

DIRECTIONS: Pre-heat oven @ 400°. Place oven proof dish in oven on high heat for 10 minutes, remove carefully and place asparagus in hot dish . Place back in oven on high for 10 minutes until roasted, turning occasionally. Place on platter and sprinkle with balsamic vinegar and coarse salt.

*"coarse" salt is also known as Kosher salt, found in the spice aisle of the grocery store.

Spicy Biscuits

any biscuit mix
1 cup cheddar cheddar cheese (grated)
2 tsp minced garlic
1 tbsp parsley
½ cup sour cream
¼ cup butter (melted)
dash of hot sauce or cayenne pepper
salt & pepper (to taste)

DIRECTIONS: Make biscuits according to directions on box, add sour cream, parsley, garlic, cheese, hot sauce. Mix well. Place in large spoonfuls (about ½ cup) on baking sheet. Bake @ 350° for 18 to 20 minutes, until lightly browned. Immediately out oven brush melted butter on top lightly and sprinkle with course salt.

Chocolate Mousse with Berries

1 pkg chocolate pudding (cooked)
1½ cups whipped cream
1 (4oz) dark chocolate bar (melted)
½ cup fresh berries (desired choice)

DIRECTIONS: Cook pudding according to directions on box, set aside and let cool. Melt chocolate bar and let cool down. Fold melted chocolate bar into whip cream. Add whipped cream to pudding. Spoon into parfait glass and top with fresh berries. Chill.

SERVES 3-4.

* Ready-made pudding in carton can also be used.

Chapter Twelve

My First Turkey Dinner!

1. Turkey or Ham

2. Stuffing

3. Mashed Potatoes

4. Broccoli Casserole

5. Corn Casserole

6. Fruit Salad

7. Relish Tray

8. Almost Pecan Pie

Turkey

DIRECTIONS: Prepare frozen turkey by thawing at least 1 day before cooking. Un- wrap turkey and remove giblets and the neck, set aside. With your hands, rub the inside cavity of the turkey with salt. Place turkey in large roasting pan (appropriate for the size of your turkey). Next, rub down the outer skin with butter or oil. Cover tightly with foil and cook according to the weight of your turkey. During this phase, the juices from the turkey can be used to baste the turkey periodically. At least one hour before turkey is done, remove foil. This will allow the turkey to brown. When the turkey is done remove from oven, let stand for at least 15 minutes covered with foil, (this allows the juices to moisten the turkey).

* Servings depend on your size of turkey.

General cooking timetable

6-9   pounds = 2½ hours
10-13   pounds = 2 hours
14-17   pounds = 3-4 hours
18-22   pounds = 4½-5 hours
22-24   pounds = 5½-6 hours

* Depending on the particular oven, watch carefully. This is just an approximate guide; You can gauge from your directions on the turkey.

Glazed Ham

1 ham, any weight, cook according to pkg directions.

My favorite glaze:
    1 cup brown sugar
    1 tbsp vinegar
    2 tsp Dijon or yellow mustard

DIRECTIONS: Pour half of the glaze over ham and bake. Pour remaining glaze over ham 15 minutes before removing from oven to serve. This allows glaze to melt onto ham.

Turkey Stuffing

1½ cube butter
giblets from turkey
1 onion
4 cups water
4 (6 oz) bags seasoned croutons (for stuffing, not salad)
2 cups celery (chopped)

DIRECTIONS: Heat 4 cups water in a large sauce pan. Add giblets, neck and onion (cut into large slices). In sauce pan put 2 tbsp butter and melt. Add celery and cook until softened. Add to water and giblets. At this time, add 1 stick butter and slow cook on low for 30 minutes. After giblet mixture is done cooking, remove the neck and any bones. Blend in blender then pour over croutons in a large bowl. Be sure to discard the neck and any bones. You may add chicken broth for flavor if dressing is too dry. Put in casserole dish and bake @ 350° until top is slightly browned, about 35-40 minutes.

SERVES 8-10.

Mashed Potatoes

10 potatoes (peeled & cut in half)
1 cube butter
½ to 1 cup milk or cream
salt & pepper

DIRECTIONS: Boil potatoes until tender and drain. Place potatoes and butter in a large bowl, add milk small amounts at a time. Use a potato masher or mixer to mash potatoes to the consistency you desire, add salt & pepper to taste.

GRAVY: In a skillet, use the drippings from the turkey and heat to a boil, slowly add milk and flour (equal parts & pre-mixed), whisk briskly to prevent any lumps. The gravy should start to thicken as you continue to whisk. If you like thinner gravy you can add a little beef broth or water, salt & pepper to taste.

Broccoli Casserole

2 (10 oz) bags frozen broccoli cuts
2 medium onions (chopped)
4 tbsp butter
4 tbsp flour
2 cups milk
salt & pepper
1 (8 oz) pkg cream cheese (softened)

DIRECTIONS: Cook broccoli and onions together in a saucepan until soft. Drain and place in a large bowl. Melt butter, add flour and make a paste, stirring constantly, add milk, salt and pepper and cream cheese, heat until cream cheese has melted. Pour over broccoli and onions, mix well. Place in baking dish and bake @ 350° for 30 minutes.

SUGGESTION: I like to put a topping of cracker crumbs and sharp cheddar cheese on top. Or, in a skillet melt ½ cup (1 cube) butter. Add 1½ cups crushed savory crackers; mix and top on casserole.

Corn Casserole

2 cans creamed corn
1⅓ cups soda crackers (crushed)
½ tsp garlic salt
salt & pepper (to taste)
2 whipped eggs

DIRECTIONS: Mix all ingredients together in a bowl, except egg. Whip eggs and add to corn mixture. Place in covered baking dish and bake @ 350° for 30 minutes.

SERVES 4-6.

Fruit Salad

This is a basic fruit salad. It consists mainly of your personal choice of fruit combinations. Just remember to have a balance with colors, textures and a flavor variety. Top with whipped topping, or the "fruit dip" (seen in chapter 9) makes a nice topping as well.

Relish Tray

Basic tray:
Pickles (dill & sweet)
olives (green & black)
marinated asparagus
assorted pickled vegetables
celery sticks
marinated mushrooms
Porcini peppers

DIRECTIONS: Relish trays can be made up of any small vegetables you like.
Just be creative.

Almost Pecan Pie

1 cup brown sugar
½ cup white sugar
1 tbsp flour
½ cup melted butter (1 cube)
2 eggs
2 tbsp evaporated milk
1 tsp vanilla
1 cup walnuts (chopped)

DIRECTIONS: Melt butter set aside to cool. When butter is cooled, mix all other ingredients. Pour into an (un-baked) pie shell. Bake @ 375°, about 30 to 45 minutes. When the pie is nicely browned and does not "jiggle" in the center it is "set". This is an indication the pie is done. Baking time will differ for individual ovens, it may take longer to bake in your oven than it does mine.

Setting the Table
(casual)

Water /Wine Glass

Salad Plate/ Bread

Salad Fork Dinner Fork Dessert Fork Dinner PLate Dinner Knife Soup Spoon

Dessert Spoon >

My Favorites

and

Family Recipes

Recipe for: _____

_____
_____
_____
_____
_____
_____
_____
_____
_____
_____
_____
_____
_____
_____
_____
_____
_____
_____
_____
_____
_____
_____
_____
_____
_____
_____
_____
_____
_____

Bake @ _____ Serves: _____

Recipe for: _____

_____

_____

_____

_____

_____

_____

_____

_____

_____

_____

_____

_____

_____

_____

_____

_____

_____

_____

_____

_____

_____

_____

_____

_____

_____

Bake @ _____ Serves: _____

Recipe for: _____
_____
_____
_____
_____
_____
_____
_____
_____
_____
_____
_____
_____
_____
_____
_____
_____
_____
_____
_____
_____
_____
_____
_____
_____

Bake @ _____ Serves: _____

Recipe for: _____
_____
_____
_____
_____
_____
_____
_____
_____
_____
_____
_____
_____
_____
_____
_____
_____
_____
_____
_____
_____
_____
_____
_____
_____
_____
_____

Bake @ _____ Serves: _____

Recipe for: _____
_____
_____
_____
_____
_____
_____
_____
_____
_____
_____
_____
_____
_____
_____
_____
_____
_____
_____
_____
_____
_____
_____
_____
_____
_____

Bake @ _____ Serves: _____

Recipe for: _____

_____

_____

_____

_____

_____

_____

_____

_____

_____

_____

_____

_____

_____

_____

_____

_____

_____

_____

_____

_____

_____

_____

_____

_____

_____

_____

Bake @ _____ Serves: _____

Recipe for: _____

_____

_____

_____

_____

_____

_____

_____

_____

_____

_____

_____

_____

_____

_____

_____

_____

_____

_____

_____

_____

_____

_____

_____

_____

Bake @ _____ Serves: _____

Our Little Cooking Secrets

1. Add 1 can of milk to tomato soup (instead of water) to make creamy tomato soup.

2. Roll equal amounts of butter and flour into small balls. Freeze them. Drop into soups ands stews and sauces to thicken.

3. We've found that bread heels don't go over very well at our house. I freeze them until I have enough to feed the ducks.

4. Rub a raw potato on the barbeque before grilling a salmon—the fish will not stick.

5. Coffee ice cubes — Pour leftover coffee into an ice cube tray and freeze.

6. Leftover cold coffee makes a great iced mocha. Add a little cream and some chocolate syrup. Pour over coffee ice cubes.

7. Equal parts of your favorite spices combined in a shaker makes a quick way to spice up your meals.

8. Mix equal parts salt & pepper together in a shaker.

9. When you make pancakes make extra, wrap individually and freeze; then place in microwave for a quick breakfast with no fuss.

10. Freeze flavored drink mixes in ice cube trays for a easy treat for kids to have on a hot day.

11. We love to buy seedless grapes and freeze them for a fun snack when it's summer time.

12. Combine bologna, mayonnaise, and dill pickle together into the blender, blend. This is a great spread for crackers or a easy snack after school.

13. If your soup is too hot and you're tired of waiting for your soup to cool, place an ice cube into the soup and it will cool shortly. (This is more for little kids in mind).

14. When cooking your pasta place a clove of garlic in the water. It gives a nice flavor to the noodles.

~ My Family Secrets and Hints ~

~ My Family Secrets and Hints ~